NEW
TESTAMENT
SURVEY

NEW TESTAMENT SURVEY

REVISED EDITION

by
Kevin Conner & Ken Malmin

Published by City Bible Publishing
9200 NE Fremont
Portland, Oregon 97220

Printed in U.S.A.

City Bible Publishing is a ministry of City Bible Church, and is dedicated to serving the local church and its leaders through the production and distribution of quality materials.

It is our prayer that these materials, proven in the context of the local church, will equip leaders in exalting the Lord and extending His kingdom.

For a free catalog of additional resources from City Bible Publishing please call 1-800-777-6057 or visit our web site at www.citybiblepublishing.com.

New Testament Survey
© Copyright 1975 by City Bible Publishing
All Rights Reserved

ISBN 0-914936-22-0

INTRODUCTION

It is of utmost importance that the Bible student obtain a good grasp of the Bible as a whole. However, in order to do so he must first gain an understanding of each book that makes up The Book. This text has been designed to be of help in this process of understanding the parts and relating them to the whole.

The format of this book is quite simple. It is designed to give a patterned glimpse of each book of the New Testament. This has been done by applying these ten points to each book: (1) Titles, (2) Author, (3) Date, (4) Key Words and Phrases, (5) Key Verses, (6) Purpose, (7) Message, (8) Outline, (9) Summary, and (10) Christ Seen. The following is an explanation of each of the ten points.

1. TITLES:

Under this heading you will find basically three things: First, the meaning of the title of the book is given (e.g. Matthew means "gift of God"). Next, alternate titles are listed when significant. Last, a distinct title has been suggested for each book. This title is meant to both describe the content of the book and to distinguish it from the other books of the Bible (e.g. Matthew is called The Book of The King because it presents Jesus as the Kingly Messiah and deals with things pertaining to the Kingdom of Heaven, a key word).

2. AUTHOR:

Under this heading is listed the author of the book. In cases where the book does not name its author, the most probable author from our point of view has been given. You will also find a brief point or two distinguishing the author and pointing out any other books written by him.

3. DATE:

Under this heading you will find under the historical books first a reference to the number of years that pass during the accounts given in the book. Then for every book an approximate date has been given as to when the book was written. Also on the Pauline Epistles information has been given to relate those epistles to the book of Acts. (There are many differences of opinion concerning the dates when the New Testament books were written. Thus, the dates listed in this text are conservative estimates.)

4. KEY WORDS AND PHRASES:

Under this heading you will find words and phrases that are keys to understanding the book at hand. These have been chosen on the basis of frequency of usage in relation to usage in other books of the Bible. These tabulations are based upon the King James Version unless otherwise noted. These words can be used for good word/theme studies in their respective books.

5. KEY VERSES:

Under this heading you will find verses that express the main subject, theme, or message of the book.

6. PURPOSE:

Under this heading you will find statements that answer the question, "Why was this book written?". These lend insight into the importance of each book. It must be considered that there are many different types of reasons why a book is written (e.g. for historical, instructional, prophetical, etc. reasons). Those thought most important have been included.

7. MESSAGE:

Under this heading you will find, with some exceptions, the statements of principle that are taught by each book as a whole or at least by a major portion of it. Of these sort of statements there could be no end but once again only those felt most significant have been included.

8. OUTLINE:

Under this heading you will find a brief, condensed outline of each book showing its structure and arrangement.

9. SUMMARY:

Under this heading you will find a paragraph description of the book, pointing out its subject and its relation to other books of the Bible, as well as other facts of interest concerning the book or its author.

10. CHRIST SEEN:

Under this heading you will find a brief description of some ways in which Christ can be seen in the book, sometimes accompanied by Scripture references supporting them.

ANY CORRESPONDENCE CONCERNING THIS TEXT MAY BE DIRECTED TO :

Ken Malmin
Portland Bible College
9201 N.E. Fremont
Portland, Oregon 97220
U.S.A.

THE BOOKS OF THE NEW TESTAMENT

1.	MATTHEW	THE KING
2.	MARK	THE SERVANT
3.	LUKE	THE PERFECT MAN
4.	JOHN	THE SON OF GOD
5.	ACTS	THE HOLY SPIRIT
6.	ROMANS	JUSTIFICATION
7.	I CORINTHIANS	N.T. CHURCH ORDER
8.	II CORINTHIANS	APOSTOLIC QUALIFICATION
9.	GALATIANS	CHRISTIAN LIBERTY
10.	EPHESIANS	THE CHURCH
11.	PHILIPPIANS	JOY AND REJOICING
12.	COLOSSIANS	THE HEAD OF THE BODY
13.	I THESSALONIANS	THE SECOND COMING OF CHRIST IN COMING
14.	II THESSALONIANS	THE SECOND COMING OF CHRIST IN JUDGMENT
15.	I TIMOTHY	THE MINISTER - QUALIFICATIONS
16.	II TIMOTHY	THE MINISTER - DOCTRINE
17.	TITUS	THE MINISTER - GODLINESS
18.	PHILEMON	RECONCILIATION
19.	HEBREWS	CHRIST'S PRIESTHOOD
20.	JAMES	FAITH AND WORKS
21.	I PETER	SUFFERING AND GLORY
22.	II PETER	TRUE KNOWLEDGE
23.	I JOHN	LOVE
24.	II JOHN	TRUTH - DOCTRINAL
25.	III JOHN	TRUTH - PRACTICAL
26.	JUDE	THE APOSTATES
27.	REVELATION	ULTIMATES

The Book of II

THE BOOKS OF THE NEW TESTAMENT

NEW TESTAMENT HISTORY 5	HISTORIC FOUNDATIONS 5	Matthew Mark Luke John Acts
DOCTRINAL EPISTLES 22	CHRISTIAN CHURCH EPISTLES 9	Romans I Corinthians II Corinthians Galatians Ephesians Philippians Colossians I Thessalonians II Thessalonians
	PASTORAL & PERSONAL EPISTLES 4	I Timothy II Timothy Titus Philemon
	HEBREW CHRISTIAN EPISTLES 9	Hebrews James I Peter II Peter I John II John III John Jude Revelation

MATTHEW

1. **TITLES**
   A. Matthew = gift of God; Levi = joined
   B. The Gospel According to Matthew
   C. The Book of The King

2. **AUTHOR:**
   Written by Matthew, a tax collector, who was called by Christ to be one of the twelve apostles.

3. **DATE:**
   A. Covers approximately 34 years from Christ's birth to His Ascension.
   B. Probably written between 52 and 68 A.D. before the fall of Jerusalem.

4. **KEY WORDS:**
   A. Kingdom (of heaven)..56
   B. Just, Right (eous, ness) (same Greek word) 25
   C. Fulfill (ed) 18

   KEY PHRASES:
   A. Son of Man 32
   B. Father in heaven, heavenly Father..20
   C. Which was spoken...13
   D. Son of David 9

5. **KEY VERSES: 1:1; 5:17, 18; 24:14**

6. **PURPOSE:**
   A. To show the Jews, by prophecy and fulfillment, that Jesus of Nazareth was the promised Kingly Messiah.
   B. To show the Jews' rejection of their King and His Kingdom.
   C. To give a preview of the events of this present age from Christ's Ascension to His Second Coming

7. **MESSAGE:**
   A. The Kingdom of heaven is not a materialistic kingdom governed by worldly principles neither is it a nationalistic kingdom confined to this earth.
   B. The Kingdom of God is a spiritual kingdom of heavenly character, nature, and order. It refers specifically to where the rule and reign of God is made effective by submission to the spiritual principles of the King.

8. **OUTLINE:**
   I. Preparation of the King ....Ch. 1 - 4
   II. Presentation of the Kingdom ....Ch. 5 - 10
   III. Preaching of the Kingdom ....Ch. 11 - 25
   IV. Passion of the King ....Ch. 26 - 28

9. **SUMMARY:**
   The distinctive characteristic of Matthew's Gospel is its appeal to the Jewish mind. It was probably originally written in Hebrew and contains many more Old Testament quotations than the other Gospels. It was thus meant to convince the Jews that Jesus of Nazareth was their promised Messiah. It presents the King and His Kingdom. Because of their nationalistic and materialistic concept of the Kingdom they rejected the King. Thus the Kingdom was taken from them and it became the ministry of the church (only mentioned in Matthew's Gospel) to preach the Gospel of the Kingdom to all the world.

10. **CHRIST SEEN:**
    Christ is seen as the King (2:2), the Lawgiver (Is. 33:22; Mt. 5-7), the Anointed (3:16, 17), the Son of David (1:1), and the Fulfillment of the Law and the Prophets (5:17).

MARK

1. **TITLES:**
   A. Mark = polite, shining (John Mark)
   B. The Gospel According to Mark
   C. The Book of The Servant

2. **AUTHOR:**

   Written by John Mark, who was a cousin of Barnabas and a companion of Peter. Many conclude that Mark was actually writing the "Gospel according to Peter."

3. **DATE:**
   A. Covers approximately 4 years from John's ministry to the beginning of the ministry of the early church.
   B. Probably written between 55 and 68 A.D.

4. **KEY WORDS:**
   A. Straightway, Immediately, Forthwith, Anon, As Soon (same Greek word) 42
   B. Multitude, People, Press (same Greek word) 38
   C. Gospel(s) 8

5. **KEY VERSE: 10:45**

6. **PURPOSE:**
   A. To present Jesus of Nazareth as the perfect and faithful Servant of Jehovah.
   B. To show to the Romans that Jesus was the Servant acting under the authority of Jehovah, giving immediate and full obedience to all commandments.

7. **MESSAGE:**
   A. The way to be great in the Kingdom of God is to be servant of all.
   B. He that humbleth himself under the hand of God shall be exalted in due time (1 Peter 5:6).

8. **OUTLINE:**
   I. The Separation of the Servant ....1:1 - 13
   II. The Service of the Servant ....1:14 - 8:30
   III. The Sacrifice of the Servant ....8:31 - 15:47
   IV. The Session of the Servant ....16:1 - 20

9. **SUMMARY**

   The distinctive characteristic of Mark's Gospel is its appeal to the Roman mind. It was probably written in Rome and contains more Latinisms than the other Gospels. Jewish customs, places, coins, and Aramaic expressions are explained, which would be necessary in order for the Roman mind to comprehend them. Mark's Gospel presents the Servant - Son as a man of action, of deeds more than words, recording more miracles than any other Gospel. It opens with the presentation of the Servant and closes with the Servant being made Lord (Mk. 16:19; Phil. 2:6 - 11; Acts 2:36).

10. **CHRIST SEEN:**

    Christ is seen as the Son of God (1:1) who became the Son of Man (10:45), the Sent-One (9:37), and the suffering Servant who after giving his life a ransom for many became the exalted Lord (16:19).

LUKE

1. **TITLES**
   - A. Luke – Luminous
   - B. The Gospel According to Luke
   - C. The Book of The Perfect Man

2. **AUTHOR:**

   Written by Luke, a physician, who was not one of the twelve apostles but was a companion of Paul. He also wrote the book of Acts.

3. **DATE:**
   - A. Covers approximately 35 years from the birth of John the Baptist to the Ascension.
   - B. Probably written between 58 and 60 A.D.

4. **KEY WORDS:**
   - A. Son 145
   - B. Kingdom (of God) 45
   - C. Preach, Publish, Proclaim, Show, Bring (3 Greek words) 20
   - D. Spirit, Holy Ghost 17

   KEY PHRASE:
   - A. Son of Man 25

5. **KEY VERSES: 4:18, 19; 19:10**

6. **PURPOSE:**
   - A. To present Jesus of Nazareth as the anointed perfect man, who after a perfect ministry provided a perfect salvation for sinful humanity.
   - B. To show to the Greeks that Jesus was God's ideal man, the only Savior.

7. **MESSAGE:**
   - A. All preaching of the Gospel must be done in the power of the Holy Spirit.
   - B. God's ideal for man is to be perfected even as His own Son.

8. **OUTLINE:**
   - I. The Preparation for/of the Son of Man ....1:1 - 4:15
   - II. The Ministry of the Son of Man ....4:16 - 21:38
   - III. The Suffering of the Son of Man ....22:1 - 23:56
   - IV. The Exaltation of the Son of Man...24:1 - 53

9. **SUMMARY:**

   The distinctive characteristic of Luke's Gospel is its appeal to the Greek mind. While the Romans had exalted strength of action, the Greeks had exalted wisdom of thought. Thus Luke draws records more of the parables of Jesus than the other Gospel writers. The portrait Luke draws of Jesus is that of the perfect man, the wisdom of God, the one who more than meets the highest ideals of the Greeks. Luke also shows Christ's relationship to the Holy Spirit. It opens with His being born of the Spirit, continues with His ministry by the power of the Spirit, and closes with His promise of the out poured Spirit.

10. **CHRIST SEEN:**

    Christ is seen as the perfect Son of Man, the Anointed Preacher, and the Savior of lost humanity (4:18, 19; 19:10).

JOHN

1. **TITLES**
   A. John – beloved
   B. The Gospel According to John
   C. The Book of The Son of God

2. **AUTHOR:**
   Written by John, a fisherman, who was one of the twelve apostles. He also wrote three epistles and The Revelation.

3. **DATE:**
   A. Covers approximately 4 years from John the Baptist's ministry to just before the Ascension.
   B. Probably written between 85 and 95 A.D.

4. **KEY WORDS:**

   A. Father (God) 122
   B. Believe (ed, est, eth, ing) 101
   C. World 80
   D. Jew (s, s') 70
   E. Love (ed, edst, est, eth)...........................57
   F. Life, Live 52
   G. True, Truth 47
   H. Witness (two Greek words) 47
   I. Son (Christ) 43
   J. Abide (Greek word) 41
   K. Verily, Verily..25
   L. Light 24

5. **KEY VERSES: 3:16; 20:31**

6. **PURPOSE:**
   A. To present Jesus Christ as the only-begotten Son of God, and to show His relationship with the Father.
   B. To show to the whole world that Jesus was sent by God the Father into the world that the world, through Him, might be saved.
   C. To show that in Jesus, God was manifested.
   D. To give a Divine interpretation of the person of Jesus Christ as to His Deity and Humanity, thus refuting prevalent heresies.

7. **MESSAGE:**
   A. The only way of approach to God the Father is through His beloved Son (Jn. 14:1, 6).
   B. There is no eternal life apart from the Son.
   C. Those who believe enter into a father and son relationship with God.
   D. Faith brings life; unbelief brings death.

8. **OUTLINE:**
   I. The Son of God ....Ch. 1:1 - 18
   II. His Public Ministry To the Jews ....Ch. 1:19 - 12:50
   III. His Private Ministry To the Disciples ....Ch. 13 - 17
   IV. His Passion To the World ....Ch. 18 - 21

9. **SUMMARY:**
   The distinctive characteristic of John's Gospel is its appeal to the whole world. Not only does John use the word "world" many times, but be also emphasizes the universal nature of Christ's mediatorship; that Jesus is the only way of salvation for the whole world. Matthew, Mark, and Luke primarily present the outer factual aspects of the Lord's life and humanity, emphasizing His public discourses and Galilean ministry. John primarily presents the inner doctrinal aspects of the Lord's life and person, emphasizing His private discourses and Judean ministry.

10. **CHRIST SEEN:**
    Christ is seen as the Word (1:1, 14), the Son (3:16), the Light (1:5), the "I AM" (8:56 - 58), and the only Way of Salvation (14:6).

ACTS

1. **TITLES:**
   A. The Acts of the Apostles
   B. The Book of The Holy Spirit

2. **AUTHORS:**
   Written by Luke, a physician, who was a companion of Paul and also wrote the Gospel bearing his name.

3. **DATE:**
   A. Covers approximately 33 years from the Ascension of Christ to the time when Paul had been a prisoner in Rome for two years.
   B. Probably written between 61 and 65 A.D.

4. **KEY WORDS:**
   A. Jew (ess, s)..81
   B. Spirit, Holy Ghost 54
   C. Gentiles, nations (same Greek word) 44
   D. Word (of God) 40
   E. Name (of Jesus, Lord) 37
   F. Pray (ed, ers, eth, ing) 35

5. **KEY VERSE: 1:8**

6. **PURPOSE:**
   A. To record Christ's continued ministry from heaven of all that He began to do and teach on earth (1:1).
   B. To give a panoramic view of the birth, formation, and development of the early church.
   C. To show the pattern by which Christ builds His church.

7. **MESSAGE:**
   A. The church, as the body of Christ, cannot function apart from the ministry of the Holy Spirit.
   B. Only by the power of the Holy Spirit can the great commission be fulfilled (Zech. 4:6).

8. **OUTLINE:**
   I. The Ministry of Peter - to the Jews - Circumcision ....Ch. 1 - 12
      Jerusalem / Judea / Samaria
   II. The Ministry of Paul - To the Gentiles - Uncircumcision ....Ch. 13 - 28
      Uttermost Parts of the Earth

9. **SUMMARY:**
   In the Gospels, Christ is presented in His earthly ministry, but in the Acts He is presented in His heavenly ministry, building His Church, as He promised (Mt. 16:18), through the power of the Spirit. In the Acts we see the order of witness in the great commission being fulfilled; first in Jerusalem, then Judea, Samaria, and the uttermost parts of the earth. The Book of Acts centers basically around two apostles; Peter, the apostle to the Jews and Paul, the apostle to the Gentiles (Gal. 2:8). It sets forth the formation and establishment of the church upon the foundational principles of the apostles' doctrine, and thus it becomes a pattern-book for the church, both universal and local.

10. **CHRIST SEEN:**
    Christ is seen as the Head of the Church, governing, guiding, equipping, and building it by the Spirit.

ROMANS

1. **TITLES:**
   A. The Epistle to the Romans
   B. The Gospel According to Paul (16:25)
   C. The Book of Justification

2. **AUTHOR:**
   Written by Paul, the apostle to the Gentiles.

3. **DATE:**
   Probably written between 55 and 58 A.D. during Paul's second visit to Corinth.

4. **KEY WORDS:**
   A. Law 78
   B. Righteousness (42); Justification (22) (related Greek words)................................64
   C. Faith (39); Believe (21) (same Greek root) 60
   D. Sin (ned, ner, s) 57
   E. Grace 24
   F. Imputed (reckoned, etc.) (one Greek word) 19

5. **KEY VERSES: 1:16, 17**

6. **PURPOSE:**
   A. To answer the age-old question, "How can a man be just before God?" (Job 9:2).
   B. To give a clear doctrinal exposition of God's method of justification by faith.
   C. To show that both Jew and Gentile are only acceptable to God through the New Covenant in Christ.

7. **MESSAGE:**
   A. The just shall live by faith (1:17).
   B. All men are under sin and cannot be justified by the works of the law.
   C. The only righteousness God accepts is a faith-righteousness based on His Word.

8. **OUTLINE:**
   I. Doctrinal: Righteousness Imputed ....Ch. 1-8
   II. National: Jew and Gentiles ....Ch. 9-11
   III. Practical: Righteousness Outworked ....Ch. 12-16

9. **SUMMARY:**
   In his epistle to the Romans Paul outlines the gospel of Christ which sets forth the righteousness of God for Jew and Gentile. In Chapters 1-3 he judges the whole world guilty under sin; the Gentiles without the law and the Jews under the law. Then in Chapters 3-8, he presents the Gospel message covering justification (3-5), sanctification (6-8), and glorification (8:18-39). In Chapters 9-11 he deals with the election (9), the rejection through unbelief (10), and the restoration (11) of the Jews through faith in Christ. In Chapters 12-16, Paul concludes his epistle by pointing out the practical duties of the justified.

10. **CHRIST SEEN:**
   Christ is seen as the Salvation of God, the Righteousness of God (10:3, 4), and the Propitiation for our sin (3:25).

I CORINTHIANS

1. **TITLES:**
   A. The First Epistle to the Corinthians
   B. The Book of Correction
   C. The Book of N.T. Church Order

2. **AUTHORS:**
   Written by Paul, the apostle to the Gentiles.

3. **DATE:**
   Probably written between 53 and 57 A.D. during Paul's stay at Ephesus on his third missionary journey (Acts 19). Later he visited Corinth again (Acts 20:1, 2).

4. **KEY WORDS:**

5. **KEY VERSES: 1:24, 30; 3:10, 11**

6. **PURPOSE:**
   A. To answer questions that the Corinthians had addressed to him concerning problems in the church (7:1; 8:1; 12:1; 16:1).
   B. To reprove and correct abuses in the mental, moral, social, and spiritual life of the Corinthian church.

7. **MESSAGE:**
   A. Recognition of the Lordship of Jesus is the solution to division in the body of Christ.
   B. God's church must be built by God's wisdom and power rather than by man's.
   C. To have order in the church we must conform to God's order.
   D. That which edifies the church is sound doctrine and that which motivates the church is God's love.

8. **OUTLINE:**
   I. Corrective Section: Carnalities ....1:1 - 8:13
      Divisions/Immorality/Marriage/Idolatry
   II. Constructive Section: Spiritualities ....9:1 - 16:24
      Ministry/Communion/Spiritual Gifts/Body of Christ/Love/Resurrection/Collections

9. **SUMMARY:**
   The church at Corinth was founded by Paul, as recorded in Acts 18. It had enjoyed the ministries of Paul, Peter, and Apollos and factions had arisen around these personalities. Other carnalities such as immorality, idolatry, and heresy had arisen. Thus Paul wrote this first epistle to reprove the Corinthians of these and to correct disorder concerning the Lord's Table, spiritual gifts, and the collection. He also answered questions and clarified misunderstanding concerning the resurrection. All of these things are evidence of a lack of spirituality, the essence of which is love.

10. **CHRIST SEEN:**
    Christ is seen as the Power of God (1:24), the Wisdom of God (1:24, 30), our Righteousness, Sanctification, and Redemption (1:30), the Love of God (13), and the Resurrection (15).

II CORINTHIANS

1. **TITLES:**
   A. The Second Epistle to the Corinthians
   B. The Book of Comfort
   C. The Book of Apostolic Qualification

2. **AUTHOR:**

   Written by Paul, the apostle to the Gentiles

3. **DATE:**

   Probably written between 54 and 57 A.D. during Paul's stay in Philippi on his third missionary journey (Acts 20).

4. **KEY WORDS:**

5. **KEY VERSES: 1:3, 4**

6. **PURPOSE:**
   A. To defend Paul's apostolic ministry and authority against false ministers trying to destroy his influence.
   B. To give further instruction concerning the collection for the saints at Jerusalem (9:1-5).
   C. To point out the need for consolation in the case of discipline mentioned in the first epistle (2:5-11).
   D. To show that the New Covenant surpasses the Old Covenant in glory.

7. **MESSAGE:**
   A. A true minister of God will glory in the Lord and not in himself.
   B. The chief purpose of church discipline is restoration rather than condemnation.
   C. Apostolic ministry is attested to by patience, signs, wonders, and mighty deeds (12:12).

8. **OUTLINE:**

9. **SUMMARY:**

   The church at Corinth had responded to Paul's first epistle dealing with certain disorders, particularly in the matter of immorality. This second epistle was written to balance out the discipline they exercised, encouraging them to restore the penitent brother back to fellowship. Whereas the first epistle was written to correct, this second epistle was written to comfort. This second epistle, like Hebrews, contrasts the glory of the New Covenant and its ministers (Christ & the Church) with the Old Covenant and its ministers (Moses & the Prophets). In the practical realm Paul reminds and exhorts the church to have the collection for the poor saints in Jerusalem ready. In the remainder of the epistle, Paul vindicates his apostleship by pointing to the fruit of his ministry.

10. **CHRIST SEEN:**

    Christ is seen as our Comforter, our Sin-offering (5:21), our Apostle, and the Glory of the New Covenant (3, 4).

GALATIANS

1. **TITLES:**

   A. The Epistle to the Galatians

   B. The Book of Christian Liberty

2. **AUTHOR:**

   Written by Paul, the apostle to the Gentiles

3. **DATE:**

   Probably written between 48 and 58 A.D. from Antioch, either at the end of Paul's first or second missionary journey (Acts 14, 18).

4. **KEY WORDS:**

5. **KEY VERSES: 3:2, 3, 11**

6. **PURPOSE:**

   A. To prove the authenticity of the Gospel according to Paul.

   B. To refute the legalism of the Judaizers under the Old Covenant.

   C. To establish the doctrine of Christian liberty under the New Covenant.

   D. To show the superiority of the Abrahamic and New Covenants over the Mosaic Covenant.

7. **MESSAGE:**

   A. True liberty in Christ is neither the legalism of the Law nor the license of the flesh.

   B. Life and righteousness come only by grace through faith.

   C. Having received the Spirit we must also walk in the Spirit.

8. **OUTLINE:**

9. **SUMMARY:**

   The Judaizers mentioned in Acts 15:1 had followed Paul's ministry among the churches of the Gentiles, having particular success in Galatia. Their teaching was a mixture of law and grace, faith and works, and Moses and Jesus. They said that a sinner was saved by faith plus works, and that the saved were to be perfected through works as they kept the Mosaic Law. The result of this teaching was that the Galatians became entangled again with the yoke of the bondage of the Law. Thus, Paul writes this epistle refuting the perverted gospel of the Judaizers and establishing the truth of his gospel. He takes up the covenant made with Abraham and by allegory he illustrates the two covenants (Mosaic Covenant and New Covenant), using Abraham's two sons, Ishmael and Isaac. Paul closes the epistle by showing that Christian liberty is neither legalism nor license.

10. **CHRIST SEEN:**

    Christ is seen as our Faith, our Righteousness, our Life, our Redeemer, the Seed of Abraham, and the New Covenant Gospel of Grace.

EPHESIANS

1. **TITLES:**
   A. The Epistle to the Ephesians
   B. The Book of the Body of Christ
   C. The Book of The Church

2. **AUTHOR:**

   Written by Paul, the apostle to the Gentiles

3. **DATE:**

   Probably written between 57 and 62 A.D. during Paul's first imprisonment at Rome (Acts 28).

4. **KEY WORDS:**

5. **KEY VERSES:** 1:22, 23; 2:6; 4:1

6. **PURPOSE:**
   A. To strengthen the believers in their love and faith in Christ.
   B. To encourage the believers to put off the old man and put on the new man.
   C. To show the unity of both Jew and Gentile in the one body of Christ.
   D. To set forth the purpose of the mystery of Christ and the church.

7. **MESSAGE:**
   A. The believer as a member of the body of Christ is seated in the heavenly places in Christ, but yet is to walk in practical love on earth.
   B. The church is a time manifestation of God's eternal purpose in Christ.

8. **OUTLINE:**

9. **SUMMARY:**

   During Paul's third missionary journey he spent at least tree years at Ephesus establishing the church. It soon became the center for the evangelization of Asia Minor. Then while imprisoned at Rome, Paul wrote this epistle. In chapter one he sets forth the eternal purpose of God in Christ and shows the heavenly calling and position of the church. Chapter three unfolds the mystery of Christ and the church. Chapter four deals with the unity of the members of the body and chapter five deals with the unity of the body with Christ under the figure of marriage. Then in chapter six Paul outlines the church's spiritual warfare. If the church had heeded Paul's admonition to walk in love they would not have received the rebuke of Christ found in Revelation 2:1-7.

10. **CHRIST SEEN:**

   Christ is seen as the Fullness of God, the Head of the Church, the Bridegroom, the Giver of Ministries, the Grace of God, and our Peace.

PHILIPPIANS

1. **TITLES:**

   A. The Epistle to the Philippians

   B. The Book of Joy and Rejoicing

2. **AUTHOR:**

   Written by Paul, the apostle to the Gentiles.

3. **DATE:**

   Probably written between 60 and 64 A.D. during Paul's first imprisonment at Rome (Acts 28).

4. **KEY WORDS:**

   A. Joy, Rejoice 18

   B. Mind (ed, s) 10

5. **KEY VERSES: 2:2; 4:4**

6. **PURPOSE:**

   A. To thank the church for their gifts and to inform them of Paul's intended visit.

   B. To warn them against the Judaizing false teachers.

   C. To exhort them to be like minded by having the mind of Christ.

   D. To encourage them to rejoice in all circumstances.

7. **MESSAGE:**

   A. The Christian life is one of joy and rejoicing which is independent of all circumstances.

   B. The key to unity (being like minded) is having the mind of Christ.

8. **OUTLINE:**

   Rejoice In:

   I. Christ our Life (1:21) ....Ch. 1

   II. Christ our Mind (2:5) ....Ch. 2

   III. Christ our Goal (3:10, 14)..Ch. 3

   IV. Christ our Strength (4:13)..Ch. 4

9. **SUMMARY:**

   The church at Philippi was founded by Paul and Silas on Paul's second missionary journey (Acts 16). Some of the first converts were gained as a result of Paul's rejoicing while in prison and it is very fitting that Paul while in prison at Rome would write an epistle of joy to this church. The theme of joy and rejoicing can be traced through the epistle as follows; Joy and Prayer (1:4-6), Joy and Opposition (1:14-18), Joy and Faith (1:25, 26), Joy and Unity (2:2), Joy and Ministry (2:14-16), Joy and Sacrifice (2:17, 18), Joy and Victory (2:25-29), Rejoicing in the Lord (3:1-3), Rejoicing Always (4:4), Rejoicing in All Circumstances (4:10-12). It is also interesting to note that faith, love, unity, and humility are seen as being at the root of joy.

10. **CHRIST SEEN:**

    Christ is seen as our Joy, our Life, our Mind, our Goal, and our Strength.

COLOSSIANS

1. **TITLES:**
   A. The Epistle to the Colossians
   B. The Book of The Head Of The Body

2. **AUTHOR:**

   Written by Paul, the apostle to the Gentiles

3. **DATE:**

   Probably written between 60 and 64 A.D. during Paul's first imprisonment at Rome (Acts 28).

4. **KEY WORDS:**
   A. Body(s) 8
   B. Fullness, Complete (Greek word) 7
   C. Wisdom 6
   D. Mystery 4
   E. Glory (ious) 4
   F. Head...3

5. **KEY VERSES: 1:18; 2:9, 10**

6. **PURPOSE:**
   A. To warn them against the heresies concerning the person and nature of Christ.
   B. To warn them against ritualism and asceticism.
   C. To present Christ as the Head of the Church in His Deity and Humanity.
   D. To exhort them to put off the old man and to put on the new man.

7. **MESSAGE:**
   A. Christ is in all, through all, and above all. He is the fullness of the Godhead bodily and the Church is complete in Him.
   B. We are to set our affections on things above and not on things on the earth.

8. **OUTLINE:**
   I. Doctrinal: The Glory of the Head ....1:1 - 2:5
   II. Practical: The Conduct of the Body ....2:6 - 4:18

9. **SUMMARY:**

   There is no record in Acts of Paul's visiting Colosse, and he evidently did not found the church there (2:1). Possibly Epaphras founded the church (1:7; 4:12, 13) which probably met in Philemon's home (4:9 with Phm. 10, 23; Phm. 2 with 4:17). According to Acts 19:10, the church was probably founded while Paul was in Ephesus only 199 miles away. Paul was well acquainted with the progress of the church and the heresies that had arisen. Thus he wrote to refute them. In section one Paul sets forth the glory and pre-eminence of Christ, refuting the heresies concerning the person and nature of Christ; in particular his pre-existence, deity and humanity. He also exhorts them to recognize the proper position of the Head over the Body. In the second section, Paul exhorts them to the practical application of the doctrine contained in the first section by putting off the old man with his deeds and by putting on the new man. The Church is seen as being complete in Christ apart from asceticism, ritualism and formalism.

10. **CHRIST SEEN:**

    Christ is seen as the Pre-existent, Preeminent, Creator, Ruler, Redeemer, Head of the Body who is the Fullness of the Godhead Bodily.

I THESSALONIANS

1. **TITLES:**

   A. The First Epistle to the Thessalonians

   B. The Book of The Second Coming of Christ in Comfort

2. **AUTHOR:**

   Written by Paul, the apostle to the Gentiles.

3. **DATE:**

   Probably written between 50 and 52 A.D. during Paul's stay at Corinth on his second missionary journey (Acts 18).

4. **KEY WORDS:**

   A. Faith, Believe...12

   B. Joy, Rejoice 7

   C. Love...6

   D. Comfort 6

   E. Coming 4

   F. Hope 4

5. **KEY VERSES: 2:19; 4:15-18**

6. **PURPOSE:**

   A. To correct mistaken views of and to establish the doctrine of the second coming of Christ

   B. To exhort the believer to display the three chief Godly virtues: faith, hope and love.

   C. To confirm the purity of Paul's ministry among the Thessalonians.

7. **MESSAGE:**

   A. The coming of Christ for his people is a comfort to those who look and patiently wait for Him.

   B. The doctrine of the second coming is a great incentive to holiness.

   C. The Lord's return will be as a thief in the night to those that are in darkness, but will not be so to those that are in the light.

8. **OUTLINE:**

   I. The Waiting Church...Ch. 1-3

      A. Elected ....Ch. 1

      B. Persecuted ....Ch. 2

      C. Afflicted ....Ch. 3

   II. The Coming Christ ....Ch. 4-5

      A. Revelation ....Ch. 4

      B. Sanctification ....Ch. 5

9. **SUMMARY:**

   Paul laid the foundation of the church in Thessalonica on his second missionary journey (Acts 17). He experienced considerable opposition from the Judaizers and did not stay there long, but soon after departing he wrote his epistle to them. The general spiritual state of the church was good but there were several things that needed correction. In chapter one, Paul commends them for being a pattern church. In chapters two and three he reminds them of the persecution and affliction which he and they endured at the hands of the Judaizers. Then in chapters four and five he exhorts them to the practical outworking of their sanctification in spirit, soul, and body. The main theme running through the epistle is the second coming of Christ, references to which are made in each chapter (1:10; 2:19; 3:13; 4:13-18; 5:1-11, 23). Also seen throughout the epistle is the abiding trinity of faith, hope, and love.

10. **CHRIST SEEN:**

   Christ is seen as our Sanctification and our Coming Lord.

II THESSALONIANS

1. **TITLES:**
   A. The Second Epistle to the Thessalonians
   B. The Book of The Second Coming of Christ in Judgement

2. **AUTHOR:**

   Written by Paul, the apostle to the Gentiles.

3. **DATE:**

   Probably written between 50 and 52 A.D. during Paul's stay at Corinth on his second missionary journey (Acts 18).

4. **KEY WORDS:**
   A. Faith, Believe..8
   B. Love, Charity (Greek word) 6
   C. Revealed 4
   D. Command (ed)..4
   E. Coming 3

5. **KEY VERSES: 1:7-10**

6. **PURPOSE:**
   A. To give further details concerning the events surrounding the coming of the Lord.
   B. To encourage the believers in the midst of severe persecution.
   C. To command them to continue in their occupation and well doing until the coming of the Lord.

7. **MESSAGE:**
   A. The coming of Christ is a judgment upon those who know not God.
   B. The Spirit of the Anti-Christ is already at work within the world.
   C. In the light of the comings of both Christ and the Anti-Christ, the believer should now walk orderly.

8. **OUTLINE:**
   I. The Christ Avenging ....Ch. 1
   II. The Anti-Christ Deceiving ....Ch. 2
   III. The Church Working...Ch. 3

9. **SUMMARY:**

   This second epistle was written soon after the first epistle. (Refer to this same heading under I Thessalonians for Paul's relationship to this church.) The first epistle shows that they were concerned about the "dead in Christ" in relation to His second coming. The second epistle shows their concern about the suffering of the living saints in relation to Christ's second coming. In chapter one, Paul comforts them by pointing out that it is far better for them to suffer tribulation previous to Christ's coming than to suffer vengeance at His Coming. In chapter two Paul describes two of the main events that are to precede the second coming; the great falling away and the revelation of the Anti-Christ. Then in chapter three he commands them to wait patiently, to walk orderly, and to work faithfully in the light of Christ's return.

10. **CHRIST SEEN:**

   Christ is seen as the Avenger and the Coming Lord Jesus Christ.

I TIMOTHY

1. **TITLES:**
   A. Timothy = honoring God; honored of God; worshipper of God
   B. The First Epistle to Timothy
   C. The Book of The Minister - Qualifications

2. **AUTHOR:**
   Written by Paul, the apostle to the Gentiles.

3. **DATE:**
   Probably written between 61 and 65 A.D. after Paul's first imprisonment at Rome (Acts 28).

4. **KEY WORDS:**
   A. Faith, Believe (1 Greek root) 35
   B. Good 23
   C. Charge, Command (ing, ment) 11
   D. Godliness 9
   E. Doctrine (s) 9
   F. Teach (er, ers) 8

5. **KEY VERSES:** 3:15; 6:11, 12

6. **PURPOSE:**
   A. To warn against false teachers.
   B. To give instruction regarding sound doctrine.
   C. To set forth the qualifications of elders and deacons.
   D. To encourage Timothy concerning his ministry.

7. **MESSAGE:**
   A. The minister that is given to godliness will be good and faithful.
   B. The true minister will teach sound doctrine and will fulfill the charge given him.
   C. The relationship between older ministries and younger ministries is to be a "father-son" relationship.

8. **OUTLINE:**
   I.   Charge Concerning Sound Doctrine ....Ch. 1
   II. Charge Concerning Public Worship ....Ch. 2
   III. Charge Concerning Church Officers ....Ch. 3
   IV. Charge Concerning False Teachers ....Ch. 4
   V.   Charge Concerning Members of the Congregation ....Ch. 5
   VI. Charge Concerning the Minister Himself ....Ch. 6
   (by H.A. Kent)

9. **SUMMARY:**
   This book is one of Paul's four personal epistles, written to individuals rather than to churches. Timothy was probably converted under Paul's ministry at Lystra (Acts 14 with I Tim. 1:2). Seven years later he had matured spiritually so that he was "well reported of", and became Paul's traveling companion (Acts 16). In chapter one, Paul points out the necessity and responsibility of maintaining sound doctrine. Paul's exhortation in chapter two deals with prayer and the roles of men and women in public worship. Chapter three is given to the qualifications of elders and deacons and the importance of maintaining them. Chapter four shows the minister's relationship to false teachers and chapter five deals with the minister's care for the various members of the congregation. Paul closes the epistle in chapter six with a personal charge to Timothy.

10. **CHRIST SEEN:**
    Christ is seen as the Elder (Ruler), the Deacon (Servant), and the Good Teacher who was faithful to the charge given Him.

II TIMOTHY

1. **TITLES:**

   A. Timothy – honoring God; honored of God; worshipper of God

   B. The Second Epistle to Timothy

   C. The Book of The Minister - Doctrine

2. **AUTHOR:**

   Written by Paul, the apostle to the Gentiles.

3. **DATE:**

   Probably written between 63 and 68 A.D. during Paul's second imprisonment at Rome. This was his last epistle written.

4. **KEY WORDS:**

   A. Faith, Faithful, Believe (1 Greek root) 12

   B. Doctrine, Teach (er, ers) 8

   C. Word (s) 7

   D. Truth 6

   E. Ashamed 4

5. **KEY VERSES: 4:1-5**

6. **PURPOSE:**

   A. To summon Timothy to come to Rome (4:9, 11, 13, 21)

   B. To direct Timothy as to proper course of action in a time of apostasy.

7. **MESSAGE:**

   A. The true minister of Christ should not be ashamed.

   B. The true minister will be faithful in times of apostasy.

   C. The true minister will be sound in doctrine, teaching and preaching the word of truth.

8. **OUTLINE:**

   I.   Charge Concerning the Testimony of Christ ....Ch. 1

   II. Charge Concerning the Service of Christ ....Ch. 2

   III. Charge Concerning Apostasy from Christ ....Ch. 3

   IV. Charge Concerning the Word of Christ ....Ch. 4:1-5

   V. Paul's Farewell ....Ch. 4:6-22

   (by H.A. Kent)

9. **SUMMARY:**

   This was the last of Paul's four personal epistles, and was written just prior to his death (refer to the summary of I Timothy for background information concerning Timothy). In chapter one Paul exhorts Timothy not to be ashamed of Christ, His Testimony, nor His servants by using himself and Onesiphorus as examples. In chapter two he uses several illustrations to exhort Timothy to be strong in his service. In chapter three he foretells of and explicitly describes the coming apostasy. Then in chapter four he charges Timothy to preach the Word as a true minister of Christ and he closes with personal instructions and greetings. It is also worthy to note that Paul here acknowledges that the end of his life and ministry is at hand (4:6-8).

10. **CHRIST SEEN:**

   Christ is seen as the Savior (1:10), the Seed of David (2:8), the Righteous Judge (4:8), and Lord of the Heavenly Kingdom (4:18).

TITUS

1. **TITLES:**
   A. Titus – pleasant, honorable, nurse, or rearer
   B. The Epistle to Titus
   C. The Book of The Minister - Godliness

2. **AUTHOR:**

   Written by Paul, the apostle to the Gentiles.

3. **DATE:**

   Probably written between 62 and 66 A.D. after Paul's first imprisonment at Rome (Acts 28).

4. **KEY WORDS:**
   A. Good 11
   B. Work (s) 8
   C. Savior..6
   D. Sound...5
   E. Doctrine...4
   F. Teach (ers, ing) 4
   G. Godly (ness, un) 3

5. **KEY VERSES: 2:11-14**

6. **PURPOSE:**
   A. To give to Titus specific instructions as to the qualifications of elders in the churches of Crete.
   B. To show the life of godliness that is to be lived by God's grace.
   C. To exhort Titus to teach sound doctrine.

7. **MESSAGE:**
   A. The teaching of sound doctrine leads to godliness of character and to good works.
   B. True godliness is embodied not in what we say but in what we are and do.
   C. A true appreciation of the grace of God will provide motivation for good works.

8. **OUTLINE:**
   I. Godliness in the Church; Qualifications of Ministers ....Ch. 1
   II. Godliness in the Home; Character of Believers ....Ch. 2
   III. Godliness in the World; Conduct of Believers ....Ch. 3

9. **SUMMARY:**

   This book is one of Paul's four personal epistles, written to individuals rather than to churches. Titus, like Timothy, was Paul's son in the faith and became one of his traveling companions. He is not named in Acts but is referred to several times in the Pauline epistles. Titus had been left in Crete to establish and set in order the churches there (1:5). Thus Paul writes to Titus giving him instructions how to carry out his mission. Chapter one emphasizes church order, giving qualifications for elders. In chapter two, Paul exhorts Titus to teach sound doctrine, showing the godly character it produces, especially in the home. Chapter three deals with the practical realm of maintaining good works and avoiding evil. Also note that this epistle contains more references to Jesus Christ as "God our Savior" than any other New Testament book (1:3, 4; 2:10, 13; 3:4, 6).

10. **CHRIST SEEN:**

    Christ is seen as our Savior (1:3), the Grace of God (2:11), and our Redeemer (2:14).

PHILEMON

1. **TITLES:**
   A. Philemon = friendship
   B. The Epistle to Philemon
   C. The Book of Reconciliation

2. **AUTHOR:**
   Written by Paul, the apostle to the Gentiles.

3. **DATE:**
   Probably written between 57 and 62 A.D. during Paul's first imprisonment at Rome (Acts 28)

4. **KEY WORDS:**
   A. Brother..4
   B. Receive 3
   C. Love(s)...3
   D. Prisoner (fellow) 3

5. **KEY VERSES: 9, 15, 16**

6. **PURPOSE:**
   A. To persuade Philemon to receive Onesimus as a brother in the Lord rather than as a runaway slave.
   B. To inform Philemon that Paul would soon be released from prison and would visit him.

7. **MESSAGE:**
   A. We are to receive one another as Christ also has received us (Rom. 15:7)
   B. Regardless of our social position we are all brethren in the Lord.

8. **OUTLINE:**
   I. Paul's Commendation of Philemon ....v. 1-7
   II. Paul's Intercession for Onesimus ....v. 8-21
   III. Paul's Salutation ....v. 22-25

9. **SUMMARY:**
   This book is one of Paul's four personal epistles, written to individuals rather than to churches. It centers around three persons:

Philemon	The Master
Onesimus :	The Runaway Slave
Paul	The Intercessor

   Philemon, a wealthy Christian of Colosse, had apparently been robbed by a runaway slave, Onesimus (v. 10, 11, 16, 18). Onesimus fled to Rome and was there led to the Lord by Paul. Paul then intended to send him back to Philemon (v. 12, 15, 16), and wrote this epistle to intercede for him. Onesimus returned with Tychicus, who carried the letters to the Ephesians and the Colossians.

   This epistle presents a beautiful picture of the Gospel of the grace of God. God our master (Philemon) receives His runaway slaves (Onesimus) because of the intercession of the mediator (Paul).

10. **CHRIST SEEN:**
    Christ is seen as our Intercessor, and Advocate.

HEBREWS

1. **TITLES:**

   A. The Epistle to the Hebrews

   B. The Book of Christ's Priesthood

2. **AUTHOR:**

   Uncertain. Suggested authors are Luke, Apollos, Barnabas, and Paul; but the weight of historical and internal evidence points to Pauline authorship.

3. **DATE:**

   Probably written between 63 and 68 A.D. just prior to the destruction of the Temple and its services in 70 A.D. (8:4; 9:6; 10:11; 13:10).

4. **KEY WORDS:**

5. **KEY VERSE: 4:14**

6. **PURPOSE:**

   A. To wean Hebrew Christians from Judaism to Christianity and to warn them against apostasy.

   B. To present the Lord Jesus Christ in His absolute pre-eminence as the final and complete revelation of God.

   C. To set forth the Promises, Sacrifice, Priesthood, and Sanctuary of the New Covenant in Christ.

7. **MESSAGE:**

   A. The cure for spiritual relapse and apostasy is a right conception of the Glory and Work of Christ.

   B. Faith in the blood of our eternal, perfect, and heavenly priest is better than that which was shadowed forth in the Old Covenant.

8. **OUTLINE:**

9. **SUMMARY:**

   This epistle was written to Hebrew believers who were under pressure to return to Judaism. Thus it is a book of comparison and contrast, showing the Son to be better than the prophets, the angels, Adam, Moses, Joshua, and Abraham. The New Covenant with its heavenly sanctuary, Melchisedec priesthood and once for all sacrifice is better than the Old Covenant with its earthly sanctuary, Aaronic Priesthood, and continual animal sacrifices. The summary is that all these things that were involved in the earthly Zion and earthly Jerusalem were only the shadow of the heavenly Zion and heavenly Jerusalem. This epistle gives the fullest exposition and interpretation of the sanctuary service set forth in Exodus and Leviticus. Hebrews and Romans stand together as the two great doctrinal epistles of the New Testament.

10. **CHRIST SEEN:**

   Christ is seen as the Word, the Angel of Jehovah, the Last Adam, The Prophet, the True Joshua (Savior), the High Priest after the order of Melchisedec; Minister and Sacrifice of the New Covenant Sanctuary, and the Author and Finisher of all Faith.

JAMES

1. **TITLES:**
   A. James = supplanter
   B. The Epistle of James
   C. The Book of Faith and Works

2. **AUTHOR:**

   Uncertain. Most scholars ascribe the authorship of this epistle to either James the son of Joseph or James the son of Alphaeus. The weight of evidence leans toward James the son of Alphaeus, who was one of the twelve apostles.

3. **DATE:**

   Probably written between 45 and 53 A.D. thus making it the first of the New Testament epistles to be written.

4. **KEY WORDS:**
   A. Faith 16
   B. Work (s) 16
   C. Law 10

5. **KEY VERSES: 2:17, 18**

6. **PURPOSE:**
   A. To comfort and encourage Hebrew believers who were going through severe trials and temptations (1:2 ; 5:8).
   B. To correct some disorders and misconceptions among the Hebrew believers' assemblies.
   C. To refute the tendency to divorce faith and works.

7. **MESSAGE:**
   A. True faith is shown by its good works.
   B. Good works are not a means to salvation, but rather are the product of salvation.
   C. Though man is not justified by the law of works, he is justified by the law of faith-works.

8. **OUTLINE:**
   I. Faith Tested and Shown by our temptations 1:1-21
   II. Faith Shown by our works ....1:22 - 2:26
   III. Faith Shown by our words 3:1-18
   IV. Faith Shown by our unworldliness 4:1-5:6
   V. Faith Shown by our patience...5:7-12
   VI. Faith Shown by our prayers 5:13-20

   (by Robert Lee)

9. **SUMMARY:**

   The apostle James became known as the bishop of the Jerusalem church. He wrote this epistle from Jerusalem "to the twelve tribes scattered abroad" (the Hebrew believers living in other lands). Rather than writing a doctrinal treatise, he wrote an epistle of practical Christian living, showing that in every area the "heart" of the matter is seen by its "fruit". He relates the principle of faith to trial, temptation, works, words, worldliness, patience, and prayers. There is no conflict between Paul and James concerning faith and works as some have suggested. Paul, in Romans, deals with justification by works after salvation (Jas. 2:20-24).

   NOTE: There is remarkable correspondence between James and the Sermon on the Mount, and there is hardly a thought that cannot be traced to Christ's personal teaching.

10. **CHRIST SEEN:**

    Christ is seen as the Lord of Glory (2:1), the Judge (4:12), the Lord of Hosts (5:4), the Husbandman (5:7), and the One who demonstrated perfect faith by perfect works.

I PETER

1. **TITLES:**
   A. Peter = stone, rock
   B. The First Epistle of Peter
   C. The Book of Suffering and Glory

2. **AUTHOR:**

   Written by Peter, a fisherman, who was one of the twelve apostles.

3. **DATE:**

   Probably written between 63 and 65 A.D.

4. **KEY WORDS:**

5. **KEY VERSES: 4:12, 13**

6. **PURPOSE:**
   A. To encourage the Christians suffering under persecution.
   B. To prepare the Christians for greater trial ahead.
   C. To show the Christians the hope of glory that lies ahead.
   D. To exhort them to fulfill practical Christian duties.

7. **MESSAGE:**
   A. God will balance out the believers' sufferings with glory and their glories with suffering.
   B. Suffering purifies and proves the believer's faith and character.
   C. Christ is the "pattern-stone" of suffering and glory.
   D. The cause of the believer's suffering should only be his godliness and not his lack of discretion.

8. **OUTLINE:**

9. **SUMMARY:**

   The apostle Peter while a disciple of Jesus had been given the initial revelation of the sufferings of Christ and the glory that should follow in the church. It is upon this experience that the themes of his epistles are built. The theme of this first epistle is glory through suffering. In the first section suffering is seen in relation to the same. The second section deals with suffering in relation to conduct, covering every area of life and setting forth Christ as the example. The final section concerns suffering in relation to attitudes in both shepherds and sheep. It should be noted that in every context where "suffering" appears "glory" is also to be found.

   NOTE: One good approach to studying the epistles of Peter is to relate his writings to his own life as revealed in the Gospels and the Acts.

10. **CHRIST SEEN:**

   Christ is seen as the Foreordained Lamb, the Chief-Cornerstone, the Stone of Stumbling, the Rock of Offence, the Example, the Chief Shepherd, and the Bishop of our Souls, who experienced the sufferings of the Cross and was crowned with Glory and Honor.

II PETER

1. **TITLES:**

   A. Peter = stone, rock

   B. The Second Epistle of Peter

   C. The Book of True Knowledge

2. **AUTHOR:**

   Written by Peter, a fisherman, who was one of the twelve apostles.

3. **DATE:**

   Probably written between 63 and 67 A.D.

4. **KEY WORDS:**

   A. Know (n, ing, eth), Knowledge 16

   B. Day(s) 12

   C. Righteous (ness) (2 Greek words) 8

   D. Judgment 4

   E. Remembrance 4

   F. Corruption (Greek word)...4

5. **KEY VERSES:** 3:17, 18

6. **PURPOSE:**

   A. To stir the saints to godliness.

   B. To warn them of false teachers and scoffers within.

   C. To contrast true and false knowledge

   D. to describe the judgments relative to the day of the Lord.

7. **MESSAGE:**

   A. True knowledge is evidenced by growth in godliness.

   B. The believer must remain pure and loyal in days of corruption and apostasy.

   C. All doctrinal and moral corruption will be judged at the day of the Lord.

8. **OUTLINE:**

   I. The Nature of True Knowledge ....Ch. 1

   II. The Peril of Abandoning True Knowledge..Ch. 2

   III. The Promise in True Knowledge ....Ch. 3

9. **SUMMARY:**

   While I Peter is built upon Matthew 16, this second epistle arises out of Peter's experience on the Mount of Transfiguration in Matthew 17. The theme of this second epistle is the contrast between true and false knowledge. In chapter one, Peter points out that the nature and character of true knowledge is expressed in Christian growth. Chapter two deals with error; stating its invasion, giving its examples, exposing its activities, and warning of its danger. In chapter three, the promise of the Coming of the Lord is confirmed and explained with emphasis on its being a day of wrath to all those who persist in false knowledge. In contrast the first epistle was written to encourage, the second to warn; the first shows the suffering and glory of the believers, the second the suffering and judgment of the unbelievers; the first emphasizes persecutions from without, the second heresies within.

   NOTE: Much of the material in chapter two is also to be found in Jude and these two passages should be studied in conjunction.

10. **CHRIST SEEN:**

    Christ is seen as the Beloved Son, the Daystar, and the Coming Lord.

I JOHN

1. **TITLES:**
   A. John = gift of God
   B. The First Epistle of John
   C. The Book of Love

2. **AUTHOR:**

   Written by John the Beloved, the author of the Gospel, three Epistles, and the Revelation.

3. **DATE:**

   Probably written between 85 and 90 A.D.

4. **KEY WORDS:**
   A. Love (d, th) 46
   B. Know (2 Greek words) 42
   C. Sin (s, ed, eth) 28
   D. World (s) 23
   E. Life 15
   F. Abide (th, ing) 12

5. **KEY VERSE: 4:16**

6. **PURPOSE:**
   A. To refute the heresy of Gnosticism born out of apostate Judaism and corrupt Paganism.
   B. To exhort the believer concerning his relationship to God, the brethren, the world, and sin.
   C. To show that true knowledge of God involves a personal relationship with Him.

7. **MESSAGE:**
   A. If we truly know God and are in fellowship with Him, then we will not love the world, but will walk in light and walk in love.
   B. If the believer abides in life he will not live in sin.

8. **OUTLINE:**
   I. God is Light ....Ch. 1, 2
   II. God is Love...Ch. 3, 4
   III. God is Life ....Ch. 5

9. **SUMMARY:**

   This epistle was born out of John's intimate relations with and his personal knowledge of the Lord Jesus as seen in his Gospel. Converts from Judaism and Paganism sought to mingle the theories of their former beliefs with the truth of the Gospel. This eventually led to the rise and development of the deadly heresy of Gnosticism. While admitting the Deity of Jesus they denied His humanity and boasted that they alone as Gnostics ("knowing ones") had the true knowledge. They despised those who maintained true apostolic doctrine. Thus John writes to assure the believers that they are the "knowing ones" having the true knowledge of Christ. In chapters one and two he applies the truth that "God is light and in Him is no darkness at all" to the believer's walk. Chapters three and four show that if a believer has true knowledge of God he will walk in love toward God and the brethren. The key thought in chapter five is "He that hath the Son hath life".

10. **CHRIST SEEN:**

    Christ is seen as the Word, the Son, our Advocate, our Propitiation, the Christ, the Light, Love, and Life.

II JOHN

1. **TITLES:**
   A. John – gift of God
   B. The Second Epistle of John
   C. The Book of Truth - Doctrinal

2. **AUTHOR:**

   Written by John the Beloved, the author of the Gospel, three Epistles, and the Revelation.

3. **DATE:**

   Probably written between 85 and 90 A.D.

4. **KEY WORDS:**
   A. Truth (s) 5
   B. Commandment (s) 4
   C. Love 4
   D. Doctrine 3
   E. Walk (ing) 3

5. **KEY VERSES: 9, 10**

6. **PURPOSE:**
   A. To warn against the deceivers that come in the spirit of the Anti-Christ.
   B. To instruct against receiving such deceivers.
   C. To encourage them to abide in the doctrine of Christ.

7. **MESSAGE:**
   A. The believer is to walk in the commandment of love and abide in true doctrine.
   B. The believer is not even to be hospitable to deceivers and transgressors of the doctrine of Christ who are anti-christs.

8. **OUTLINE:**
   I. Walking in True Doctrine ....v. 1-6
   II. Falling from True Doctrine ....v. 7-13

9. **SUMMARY:**

   This second epistle of John is either a personal epistle written to a Christian lady and her children or a church epistle written to a local church and its members. In either circumstance the truth of the epistle is intended for all believers. In the first section of the epistle John emphasizes walking in true doctrine, keeping the commandment of love. The second section gives warning concerning those who transgress true doctrine, showing that they are deceivers and anti-christs. He exhorts them not even to show hospitality to those false brethren. The basic principles in this epistle arise from the teachings of Christ found in John's Gospel.

10. **CHRIST SEEN:**

    Christ is seen as the Truth, the Son, and the Christ who is come in the flesh.

III JOHN

1. **TITLES:**
   A. John = gift of God
   B. The Third Epistle of John
   C. The Book of Truth - Practical

2. **AUTHOR:**
   Written by John the Beloved, the author of the Gospel, three Epistles, and the Revelation.

3. **DATE:**
   Probably written between 85 and 90 A.D.

4. **KEY WORDS:**
   A. Truth, True 7
   B. Receive (th) 3
   C. Walk (est)..2
   D. Love (th) 2

5. **KEY VERSE: 3**

6. **PURPOSE:**
   A. To encourage Gaius in his reception of the brethren.
   B. To assure Gaius that John himself would deal with the arrogant Diotrephes when he next visited the church.
   C. To bear record of Demetrius' good report in the truth.

7. **MESSAGE:**
   A. Believers must be willing to receive the brethren and show hospitality to them.
   B. Any leader who desires to have the pre-eminence will by his deeds bring himself under divine discipline.
   C. Christianity is a practical walk in truth and love.

8. **OUTLINE:**
   I. Exhortation - Gaius ....v. 1-8
   II. Condemnation - Diotrephes ....v. 9-11
   III. Commendation - Demetrius ....v. 12-14

9. **SUMMARY:**
   This third epistle of John is a personal epistle written to Gaius. In the early church there were various believers called to itinerant ministry. Having no guarantee of material support they were dependent on the hospitality of the Christians in the cities in which they ministered. John had sent certain brethren and had written to the church to receive them, but Diotrephes, a leader in the church, refused to receive them. He manifested an arrogant, domineering spirit by threatening with excommunication any members who would receive them. Thus John writes concerning this situation commending Gaius for receiving them and assuring him that he would deal with the matter personally upon his arrival. This epistle centers around three men, showing their relation to truth and love:

   Gaius ....well beloved, kind, generous, hospitable
   Diotrephes...arrogant, autocratic, domineering
   Demetrius ....well-reported commendable

   While II John warns against receiving false teachers who deny the doctrine of Christ, III John warns against refusing to receive those who are true ministers of Christ.

10. **CHRIST SEEN:**
    Christ is seen as the Truth.

JUDE

1. **TITLES:**
   A. Jude – praise
   B. The Epistle of Jude
   C. The Book of The Apostates

2. **AUTHOR:**
   Uncertain. Most authors ascribe the authorship of this epistle to either Jude the son of Joseph or Jude the son of Alphaeus. The weight of evidence leans toward Jude the son of Alphaeus, who was one of the twelve apostles and the brother of James (see James).

3. **DATE:**
   Probably written between 67 and 80 A.D.

4. **KEY WORDS:**
   A. Ungodly 6
   B. Kept (Greek word)..5
   C. Eternal, Forever 4

5. **KEY VERSE: 3**

6. **PURPOSE:**
   A. To exhort believers to contend for the faith.
   B. To warn them of apostate teachers and to expose their character, doctrine and deeds by example and illustration.
   C. To comfort them in view of apostasy.

7. **MESSAGE:**
   A. True believers in the midst of apostasy must contend for the faith.
   B. All the ungodly will be brought to eternal judgment by fire.
   C. God is always faithful to keep his elect form falling.

8. **OUTLINE:**
   I. Contending For the Faith ....v. 1-4
   II. Apostasy From the Faith ....V. 5-16
   III. Keeping the Faith ....v. 17-25

9. **SUMMARY:**
   Jude opens his epistle by commenting that he had intended to write concerning "the common salvation" but that he was constrained by the spirit to write concerning a different matter. False teachers had crept in, denying the faith and giving birth to apostasy in the church. Jude, then , exhorts the believers to contend for the faith. He exposes the false teachers by using examples from history and illustrations from nature and then he foretells of their certain judgment at the Lord's coming. Lastly he exhorts and encourages the believers concerning their remaining steadfast in the faith.

   NOTE: This is the only book that refers to the contention over the body of Moses and the prophecy of Enoch.

   NOTE: Much of the material in Jude is also to be found in II Peter and these two passages should be studied in conjunction.

   NOTE: This epistle is made up of triads.

10. **CHRIST SEEN:**
    Christ is seen as the coming Lord, the Judge and "The Only Wise God, our Savior".

REVELATION

1. **TITLES:**
   A. The Revelation
   B. The Apocalypse
   C. The Book of Ultimates

2. **AUTHOR:**
   Written by John the Beloved, the author of the Gospel, three Epistles.

3. **DATE:**
   Probably written between 90 and 96 A.D.

4. **KEY WORDS:**

A. Angel (s, 's)	76	H. King (s, dom)	30
B. See, saw (est)	65	I. Book (s)	30
C. Seven (th)	59	J. Lamb ('s)	29
D. Hear (d, eth)	46	K. Spirit (s)	22
E. Throne (s)	40	L. Church (es)	20
F. Name (s, 's)	36	M. White	19
G. Twelve, Twenty-four	30		

5. **KEY VERSE: 1:19**

6. **PURPOSE:**
   A. To give a revelation of the Lord Jesus Christ in the glory of His varied offices.
   B. To give instruction, encouragement and rebuke to the seven local churches in Asia.
   C. To give to the universal church a prophetic panorama of events from the First to the Second Coming of Christ.
   D. To bring into focus the ultimate conclusion of the plan of redemption which was begun in Genesis, the book of Creation.

7. **MESSAGE:**
   A. The Kingdom of God will ultimately and completely triumph over all evil.
   B. Those who overcome the world, the flesh, and the devil will receive everlasting rewards.
   C. A true witness must be able to testify of that which he has seen and heard.

8. **OUTLINE:**
   I. Things Seen - The Glorified Christ...Ch. 1
   II. Things Which are - The Ministering Christ ....Ch. 2, 3
   III. Things Hereafter - The Triumphant Christ ....Ch. 4-22

9. **SUMMARY:**
   John was in exile on the Isle of Patmos. There, while caught up in the spirit, he was given a series of visions showing the progressive unfolding of events from the Fist Coming through to the New Heavens and New Earth. The first three chapters show Christ's relationship to His church, local and universal. The remainder of the book deals with the following subjects; the seven-sealed books (Rev. 4-7), the seven trumpets (Rev. 8-11), the tribulation (Rev. 12-14), the seven vials (Rev. 15, 16), Mystery Babylon (Rev. 17, 18), the Second Coming, the Kingdom and the New Heavens and New Earth (Rev. 19-22). All that began in Genesis pertaining to the Old Creation, finds its consummation in Revelation which then introduces the New Creation.

10. **CHRIST SEEN:**
    Christ is seen as the Head of the Church, the Lamb, the Lion of the Tribe of Judah, the Jehovah Angel, the Bridegroom, the Word, and the King of Kings and the Lord of Lords.

HISTORICAL BACKGROUND

FROM THE OLD TESTAMENT
THROUGH THE NEW TESTAMENT

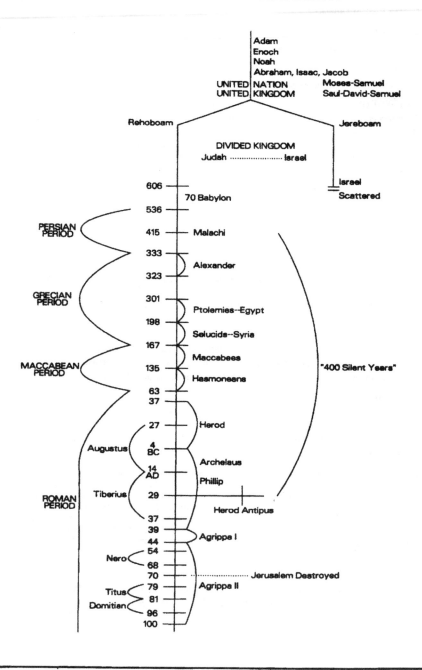

Adam
Enoch
Noah
Abraham, Isaac, Jacob

UNITED | NATION   Moses-Samuel
UNITED | KINGDOM   Saul-David-Samuel

Rehoboam   Jereboam

DIVIDED KINGDOM
Judah .... Israel

Israel
Scattered

606
70 Babylon

536

PERSIAN PERIOD

415 — Malachi

333

Alexander

323

GRECIAN PERIOD

301 — Ptolemies--Egypt

198 — Selucids--Syria

167 — Maccabees

135 — Hasmoneans   "400 Silent Years"

MACCABEAN PERIOD

63
37

27 — Herod

Augustus   4 BC

Archelaus

14 AD

Phillip

Tiberius   29

Herod Antipus

ROMAN PERIOD

37
39
44 — Agrippa I
54

Nero   68
70 .... Jerusalem Destroyed
Titus   79 — Agrippa II
81
Domitian   96
100

THE AUTHORS OF
THE NEW TESTAMENT

NATIONALITY	AUTHOR	MINISTRY OCCUPATION	BOOK
Jew	Matthew	Apostle, Tax-collector	Matthew
Jew/Roman	Mark	Missionary, Disciple of Peter	Mark
Greek	Luke	Disciple of Paul, Physician	Luke , Acts
Jew	John	Apostle, Fisherman	John, I John, II John, III John, Revelation
Jew	James	Apostle?	James
Jew	Jude	Apostle?	Jude
Jew	Peter	Apostle, Fisherman	I Peter, II Peter
Jew	Paul	Apostle, Tentmaker, Pharisee	Romans, I Corinthians, II Corinthians, Galatians, Ephesians, Philippians, Colossians, I Thessalonians, II Thessalonians, I Timothy, II Timothy, Titus, Philemon, Hebrews?

THE BACKGROUND
FOR PAULINE EPISTLES

BACKGROUND FOR	CITIES	ACTS REFERENCE
Galatians	Antioch, Iconium, Lystra, Derbe	Acts 13:14-14:28
Philippians	Philippi	Acts 16:11-40
I & II Thessalonians	Thessalonica	Acts 17:1-9
I & II Corinthians	Corinth	Acts 18:1-16
Ephesians	Ephesus	Acts 19:1-41; 20:17-38; 20:17-38

BOOK	WHERE WRITTEN	ACTS REFERENCE
Galatians	Antioch	Acts 14
I & II Thessalonians	Corinth	Acts 18
I Corinthians	Ephesus	Acts 19
II Corinthians	Macedonia	Acts 20:1, 2
Romans	Corinth	Acts 20:2
Colossians		
Philemon	Rome	Acts 28:30
Ephesians		
Philippians		
I Timothy		
Titus		
II Timothy	Rome after "Acts imprisonment"	
Hebrews		

THE UNFOLDING REVELATION IN THE EPISTLES

In the New Testament we find that the epistles are built upon the foundation of the gospels and Acts. The purpose of this supplement is to point out how the key subjects of the epistles find their basis in the four gospels. Through the gospels we come to know Christ after the Spirit. While the gospels declare historical facts, the epistles interpret those facts in setting forth doctrine.

GOSPELS	EPISTLES
Christ after flesh	Christ after Spirit
Declare	Interpret
History	Doctrine

EPISTLE	KEY SUBJECTS	GOSPEL BASIS
Romans	Justification By Faith	Jn. 3:16
I & II Corinthians	N.T. Church Order	Mt. 16:18
Galatians	Law & Grace; Liberty	Mk. 14:24; Jn. 8:36
Ephesians	The Body; Church-Eternal Purpose	Mt. 16:18
Philippians	Joy & Rejoicing	Jn. 15:11
Colossians	The Head (Majesty of Christ)	Mt. 28:19,20
I & II Thessellonians	2nd Coming; Anti-Christ	Jn. 14:1-3
Timothy, Titus	Pastoral Epistles; Elders & Deacons	Lk. 11:49; Mt. 23:34
Philemon	Reconciliation	Mt. 5:24; 18:15
Hebrews	Christ's Priesthood; Perfection	Mk. 10:45; Mt. 5:48
James	Faith & Works	Mt. 5-7
I Peter	Suffering & Glory; Church	Mt. 16:18, 21, 27
II Peter	2nd Coming; False Prophets	Mt. 24
I, II, III John	Love, Light, Life; Anti-Christ	Jn. 1, 6, 11, 13
Jude	The Acts of the Apostates	Mt. 24
Revelation	2nd Coming; Ultimates	Lk. 19:11-27; Jn. 5:29

"But the word of the Lord was unto them precept upon precept, line upon line, here a little, and there a little." Isaiah 28:13

"I have yet many things to say unto you, but ye cannot bear them now...when the Spirit of Truth is come, He will guide you into all Truth..." John 16:12, 13

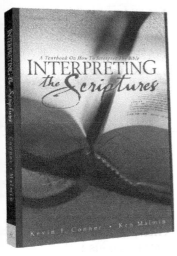
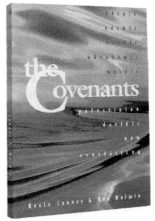
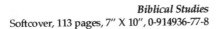

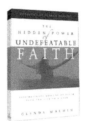

Recent Releases from
CITY BIBLE PUBLISHING

FAX: 503.257.2228 • EMAIL: order@CityBiblePublishing.com

The Power of Spiritual Alignment
Living According to the Seven Firsts of Jesus
Frank Damazio
ISBN 1-886849-87-0

The Hidden Power of a Surrendered Life
Compelling Lessons from the Life of Esther and Others
Frank Damazio
ISBN 1-886849-82-X

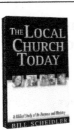

The Local Church Today
A Biblical Study of Its Purpose and Ministry
Bill Scheidler
ISBN 0-914936-04-2

Apostles: The Fathering Servant
A Fresh Biblical Perspective on Their Role Today
Bill Scheidler & Dick Iverson
ISBN 1-886849-81-1

Truths That Build
Principles that Will Establish & Strengthen the People of God
Dick Iverson
ISBN 1-886849-80-3

Great Faith
Making God Big
Wendell Smith
ISBN 1-886849-79-X

The Making of a Vision
Seeing the Invisible, Believing the Impossible, Overcoming the Obstacles
Frank Damazio
ISBN 1-886849-90-0

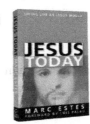

Jesus Today
Living Life as Jesus Would
Marc Estes
ISBN 1-886849-76-5

Empowering Your Preaching
Frank Damazio

Student Handbook	*Audio - 5 Cassettes*
ISBN 1-886849-91-9	UPC 1-886849-92-7

Empowering the Giving of Your Church
Frank Damazio

Student Handbook	*Audio - 5 CDs*	*Audio - 5 Cassettes*
ISBN 1-59383-012-2	UPC 643101-118221	UPC 643101-118344

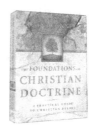